THE BOOK OF ICES.

ESTABLISHED 1883.

Telephones:
3115 } MUSEUM.
6045 }

Telegrams:
" MARSHALL'S COOKERY,
WESTDO, LONDON."

MARSHALL'S
SCHOOL OF COOKERY,

The oldest established, largest, and most successful
School of Cookery of its kind in the World.   Specially
established for high-class French and English Cookery.

32-30, Mortimer St., London, W.1.

OFFICE HOURS 10 to 5.   SATURDAYS 10 to 1.

CLASS FEES.

(Payable in advance, or on admission.)

Per day, Half Guinea.   6 days' course, £2 15s.

12 days' course, 5 Guineas.   24 days' course, 9 Guineas.

Seven weeks' course, 35 Lessons, 12 Guineas.

Three months' course, 60 Lessons, 20 Guineas.

Fees are inclusive of all materials used, and pupils do practical work.

Pupils can join any day.   Course Pupils need not attend consecutive days, but any time within two years.

CLASS HOURS.

Daily 11 a.m. till about 4 p.m.   Saturdays excepted.

For Programme of Work see " The Table" (page 76).

This facsimile edition published in 2018 by
GRUB STREET
4 Rainham Close
London
SW11 6SS

Email: food@grubstreet.co.uk
Twitter: @grub_street
Facebook: Grub Street Publishing
Web: www.grubstreet.co.uk

A CIP record for this title is available from the British Library
ISBN 978-1-911621-22-5

Printed and bound by 4Edge

THE BOOK OF ICES.

INCLUDING

CREAM AND WATER ICES,

SORBETS, MOUSSES, ICED SOUFFLÉS, AND

VARIOUS ICED DISHES,

WITH

NAMES IN FRENCH AND ENGLISH,

BY

A. B. MARSHALL.

(Copyright.)

REVISED AND ENLARGED EDITION.

London:

MARSHALL'S SCHOOL OF COOKERY, 32, MORTIMER STREET

PUBLISHED BY

ROBERT HAYES, LIMITED,

ROSEBERY HOUSE, BREAM'S BUILDINGS, E.C.4.

❄ PUBLICATIONS. ❄

Mrs. A. B. MARSHALL'S COOKERY BOOK

70th Thousand. 468 Pages. 125 Illustrations. Price 5s.
By Post, 5s. 9d.

Mrs. A. B. MARSHALL'S LARGER COOKERY BOOK OF EXTRA RECIPES.

Dedicated by permission to H.R.H. PRINCESS CHRISTIAN.

11th Thousand. Price 10s. 6d. Post Free, 11s. 9d.

Contains 664 large pages, with over 1200 Recipes and 284 Illustrations, including the newest Dishes in Savouries, Entrées, Sweets, &c., divided into 18 Chapters on the different branches.

Frontispiece—Portrait of Mrs. A. B. Marshall.

This Work contains no Dishes given in the smaller Volume.

THE BOOK OF ICES.

By Mrs. A. B. MARSHALL. 20th Thousand. Price 2s. 6d.
Post Free, 2s. 9d.

FANCY ICES.

By Mrs. A. B. MARSHALL. Third Thousand. 238 Pages.
86 Illustrations. Price 5s. Post Free, 5s. 9d.

For all who give Dinner Parties, Balls, Garden Parties, and other Social Gatherings, this book is for use as a second volume to the "Book of Ices."

CONTENTS.

	PAGE
HINTS ON MAKING ICES	1
FREEZING THE ICES	2
MOULDING AND KEEPING ICES	3
SACCHAROMETER	5
ICE MOULDS AND MOULDING	5
CUSTARDS FOR CREAM ICES (Nos. 1 to 4)	6
PLAIN CREAM ICE (No. 5)	7
CREAM ICES MADE FROM JAMS (Nos. 6 and 7)	7
CREAM ICES MADE FROM FRUIT AND LIQUEUR SYRUPS (Nos. 8 and 9)	8
CREAM ICES MADE FROM RIPE FRUITS, ETC.	9

10. Almond or Orgeat.
11. Apple.
12. Apricot.
13. Banana.
14. Biscuit.
15. Black Currant.
16. Brown Bread.
17. Burnt Almond.
18. Cedrat.
19. Cherry.
20. Chestnut.
21. Chocolate.
22. Cinnamon.
23. Cocoanut.
24. Coffee (brown)
25. Coffee (white).

26. Cranberry.
27. Cucumber.
28. Curaçoa.
29. Damson.
30. Filbert.
31. Ginger.
32. Gooseberry.
33. Greengage.
34. Italian Cream.
35. Kirsch.
36. Lemon.
37. Marmalade.
38. Maraschino.
39. Neapolitan or Pinachée.
40. Noyeau.
41. Orange.

PAGE

42. Orange Flower Water.
43. Peach.
44. Pear.
45. Pine-apple.
46. Pistachio.
47. Plum.
48. Quince.
49. Raspberry.
50. Ratafia.
51. Red Currant

52. Rhubarb.
53. Rice.
54. Spanish Nut.
55. Strawberry.
56. Tangarine.
57. Tea.
58. Vanilla.
59. Walnut.
60. White Wine.

FRUIT SYRUPS 27

WATER ICES 27

61. Made from Jams | 62. Made from Fruit Syrups.

WATER AND PERFUMED ICES MADE FROM RIPE FRUITS, ETC. ... 28

63. Apple.
64. Apricot.
65. Banana.
66. Bergamot.
67. Black Currant.
68. Cedrat.
69. Cherry.
70. Cranberry.
71. Damson.
72. Ginger.
73. Grape.
74. Jasmine.

75. Lemon.
76. Mille Fruits.
77. Melon.
78. Mulberry.
79. Orange.
80. Peach.
81. Pear.
82. Pine-apple.
83. Raspberry.
84. Red Currant.
85. Rose Water.
86. Strawberry.

87. SYRUP FOR WATER ICES 34

SORBETS, ETC. (Note) 35

88. Sorbet of Peaches à la Portugaise.
89. Sorbet of Strawberries.
90. Sorbet of Apricots à la Moscovite.

91. Roman Punch (1).
92. Roman Punch (2).
93. American Sorbet.
94. Rum Sorbet.

MOUSSES (Note) 38

95. Coffee Mousse.
96. Strawberry Mousse.

97. Maraschino Mousse.
98. Vanilla Mousse.

CONTENTS.

ICED SOUFFLÉS (Note) ... ... PAGE 40

99. Coffee Soufflé.
100. Vanilla Soufflé.

101. Strawberry Soufflé.
102. Coffee Soufflés in cases.

DRESSED ICES, ETC. (Note) 42

103. Strawberry and Vanilla Bombe.
104. Bombe with Fruits.
105. Sovereign Bombe.
106. Plain Ice Pudding.
107. Nesselrode Pudding.
108. Sauce for Nesselrode Pudding.
109. Chateaubriand Bombe.

110. Ginger Bombe.
111. Bartlett Pudding.
112. Plombière of Strawberries.
113. Muscovite of Oranges.
114. Muscovite of Strawberries.
115. Little Soufflés of Cheese.
116. Iced Spinach à la Crème.
117. Soufflés of Curry à la Ripon.

ASPIC JELLY 52

APPENDIX.

Ice moulds 53–62
Freezer 64
Ice Cave 65–66
Freezing Salt ... 70

Syrups 70
Colours, paste and liquid 71
Concentrated essences ... 71
Saccharometer ... 71

ALPHABETICAL INDEX 77

THE BOOK OF ICES.

HINTS ON MAKING ICES.

1. Too much sugar will prevent the ice from freezing properly.

2. Too little sugar will cause the ice to freeze hard and rocky.

3. If the ices are to be moulded, freeze them in the freezer to the consistency of a thick batter before putting them in the moulds.

4. If they are to be served unmoulded, freeze them drier and firmer, so that the ice does not run.

5. Broken ice alone is not sufficient to freeze or mould the ices ; rough ice and freezing salt must be used.

6. Fruit ices will require to be coloured according to the fruit. For Harmless Colours see p. 71.

7. When dishing up ices, whether in a pile or moulded, it will be found advantageous to dish them on a napkin or paper, as they will not conduct the heat to the bottom of the ices so quickly as the dish would.

Those who wish to be proficient can save themselves a great amount of time, trouble, and anxiety, as well as expense of materials, by attending at Marshall's School of Cookery on any day arranged for "Ices," when they will see the whole system in different branches practically taught, and be able to work from any recipes with ease.

FREEZING THE ICES.

Having prepared the cream, custard, or water ice as explained in the following recipes, take the Patent

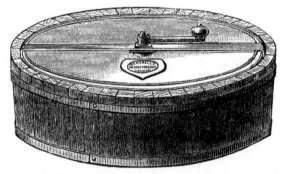

Freezer and lift the pan from the tub; put pounded ice in the tub to the depth of about 1 to 1½ inch, according to the quantity of cream, etc., to be frozen, and throw over the pounded ice half its weight of freezing or rough salt and mix it in with the pounded ice. Replace the pan on the pivot in the tub, *leave for 5 or 6 minutes to allow the freezer to become thoroughly cold, then* pour your cream, etc., into the pan through the little door in the lid, and turn the handle. Observe, there is no need to pack ice and salt *round* the pan, but merely to put it *on the bottom of the tub under the pan.* After turning the handle for 2 or 3 minutes, examine

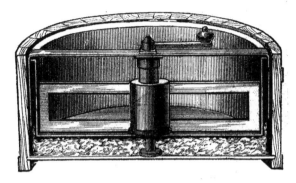

the progress of the freezing by looking through the door in the lid. When the cream is sufficiently frozen (see Hints 3 and 4, p. 1), hold the pan with one hand and unscrew the handle and lift off the crossbar and lid.

Keep the freezer clean, and when cleaning take out the mixing fan.

N.B.—The cream, etc., in the pan should never be more than 1 inch deep. The shallower the layer is in the pan the quicker it will freeze.

For description, sizes, and prices of freezers, see p. 64.

MOULDING AND KEEPING ICES.

Take a patent cave and remove the lids as shown in the annexed engraving, and fill in between the metals with a mixture of 2 parts broken ice and 1 part salt; shake it well down so that the mixture goes underneath the cupboard of the cave, and fill well up

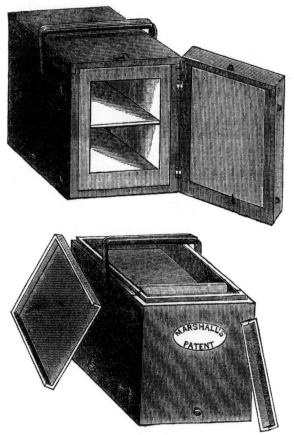

so that the lid will just slide over the ice and salt. Replace the lids and allow to stand for some 10 to 15 minutes before using.

Now fill your mould with the frozen cream from the freezer, and see that it is well pressed or shaken into the mould. Place the mould for $1\frac{1}{2}$ to 3 hours in the cave; examine from time to time if you wish. When you desire to turn the ice out of the mould, dip the mould for an instant in cold water and turn it out as you would a jelly. If you put the ice, when turned out, back into the cave and shut the door, it will keep its shape for many hours, so that ices can be prepared long before actually required; they have thus been kept from one day to another. When anything is freezing in the cave, do not open the door more often than necessary.

When the cave is done with, remove the brine and wash out with boiling water, and see that it is put away dry.

For description, sizes, and prices of caves, see p. 65.

THE SACCHAROMETER.

This is an instrument for testing quantity of sugar in water ices, etc. To ensure uniform success, it is necessary that the strength of the syrups should always be the same. Instructions for using the instruments are sent with them (see p. 71). Their use is strongly recommended.

ICE MOULDS AND MOULDING.

These are to be had in almost endless variety—a list of some popular ones with prices will be found on pages 53–62.

In using ice moulds, great taste and novelty can be exercised in dishing up, and they afford to the cook the opportunity of making some of the prettiest dishes it is possible to send to the table.

CUSTARDS FOR CREAM ICES.

Never allow the *custard to boil*, or it will curdle.

Always add the flavouring when the custard is cooled, unless otherwise stated.

1.—Very Rich.

1 pint of cream, a quarter of a pound of castor sugar, and 8 yolks of eggs.

Put the cream in a pan over the fire, and let it come to the boil, and then pour it on to the sugar and yolks in a basin and mix well. Return it to the pan and keep it stirred over the fire till it thickens and clings well to the spoon, but do not let it boil; add 3 sheets of Marshall's gelatine, then pass it through a tammy, or hair sieve, or strainer. Let it cool; add vanilla or other flavour, and freeze. Mould if desired. When partly frozen, half a pint of whipped cream slightly sweetened may be added to each pint of custard.

2.—Ordinary.

Bring 1 pint of milk to the boil, then add 4 sheets of Marshall's gelatine, a quarter of a pound of castor sugar, and 8 yolks of eggs. Prepare this as in the above recipe. Flavour and freeze. This can be improved by using half a pint of milk and half a pint of cream instead of all milk.

3.—Common.

1 pint of milk, a quarter of a pound of sugar, and 2 whisked eggs. Put these in a pan and stir over the fire to *nearly* boiling. Remove it from the fire and stir in a quarter of an ounce of Marshall's gelatine (see p. 72). When the gelatine is dissolved, pass it through the tammy, or hair sieve, or strainer. Flavour and freeze as above.

4.—Un-cooked.

Half a pint of new milk, $\frac{1}{2}$ pint of cream or evaporated milk, 8 tablespoonfuls of any of Marshall's Fruit or Liqueur Syrup, colour according to flavour, add a few drops of lemon juice, and freeze. (No sugar is required.)

5.—PLAIN CREAM ICE (*Crème Glacée*).

1 pint of cream sweetened with a quarter of a pound of castor sugar. Freeze dry.

This can be served in the centre of a compote of fruits, or with fresh fruits arranged round it; or the fruits and the cream can be served on separate dishes.

6.—CREAM ICES MADE FROM JAMS.

As jams vary exceedingly in the amount of sugar they contain, it *is* most necessary that this be taken into consideration to ensure success. The following recipe is for jams of average sweetness.

Boil 1 pint of milk and then mix it into 8 raw

yolks of eggs, put this in a pan and stir over the fire until it thickens, then add 4 tablespoonfuls of jam, 4 sheets of Marshall's gelatine, and pass it through the tammy or hair sieve. When cool freeze, and when partly frozen add half a pint of whipped cream sweetened with half a teaspoonful of castor sugar. Colour the custard with a little red, green, yellow, or purple colour (p. 71) according to fruit.

7.—Another way.

Take 4 tablespoonfuls of jam as above, and the strained juice of 1 lemon and 1 pint of cream ; pass it through the tammy or hair sieve, and freeze it. Colour according to fruit.

8.—CREAM ICES MADE FROM FRUIT AND LIQUEUR SYRUPS

The syrups made by different manufacturers vary much in strength. The following recipe is for the syrups mentioned on p. 70.

Make a custard as in Nos. 1, 2, 3, or 4, without sugar, and add 4 tablespoonfuls of syrup to half a pint of custard, and freeze. Mould or serve in a pile.

9.—Another way : very simple.

Add 4 tablespoonfuls of fruit purée or liqueur syrup to half a pint of cream or milk, and colour if necessary. Freeze. Mould or serve in a pile.

CREAM ICES MADE FROM RIPE FRUITS, ETC.

10.—Almond or Orgeat Cream Ice (*Crème d'Amandes**).

Blanch, peel, and pound half a pound of sweet almonds mixed with 6 or 7 bitter ones. During the pounding add a teaspoonful of orange-flower water, 3 or 4 drops of essence of almonds, and a pint of tepid milk or cream (or half milk and half cream). Sweeten with 4 ounces of castor sugar, and add to 1 pint of custard (Nos. 1 to 4) or 1 pint of sweetened cream (No. 5). Freeze and serve in a pile on a napkin, or mould it, or serve it in meringues or in little fancy papers. Serve as a dinner or dessert ice.

11.—Apple Cream Ice (*Crème de Pommes*).

Peel and cut up 2 pounds of good cooking apples, put them on the stove in ¾ of a pint of water, a little piece of cinnamon, the peel of a lemon, the juice of one, 2 bayleaves, 6 ounces of sugar, and 3 sheets of Marshall's gelatine. Cook quickly until reduced to a purée, then pass it through the tammy cloth or hair sieve, and mix it with 1 pint of sweetened cream (No. 5) or 1 pint of custard (Nos. 1 to 4). Add a few drops of Marshall's sap green. Freeze and serve as for previous recipe. Serve as a dinner or dessert ice.

---

* The French names can be written in either of the following forms, as for Vanilla Cream Ice:—Crème à la Vanille, Crème de Vanille and the word "glacée" may be added; or Glace à la Vanille

12.—Apricot Cream Ice (*Crème d'Abricots*).

Cut 12 ripe apricots into halves, crack the stones, take out the kernels, and put the fruit to cook, for about a quarter of an hour, with 1½ pints of water and 4 ounces of loaf sugar. When tender mix a little liquid saffron or apricot yellow (p. 71) with the fruit and a few drops of vanilla, and pass it through the tammy cloth or hair sieve. Add this purée to 1½ pints of custard (Nos. 1 to 4) or to the sweetened cream (No. 5). Freeze it, then add half a pint of whipped cream and a wineglass of kirsch syrup, and finish as for previous recipes. Serve as a dinner or dessert ice.

13.—Banana Cream Ice (*Crème de Bananes*).

Peel 6 raw ripe bananas and pound them to a pulp, add the juice of 2 lemons, 2 oranges, and a glass of curaçoa (p. 70). Pass it through the tammy cloth and finish with 1 pint of sweetened cream or custard as in previous recipe. Serve as a dinner, dessert, or supper ice.

14.—Biscuit Cream Ice (*Biscuits glacés à la Crème*).

This ice can be made with the pieces of any kind of biscuit; rub them through the wire sieve and finish as for brown bread ice (No. 16). Serve as a dinner, dessert, or supper ice.

15.—Black Currant Cream Ice (*Crème de Cassis*).

Put 1 pound of ripe black currants, 6 ounces of castor sugar, half a pint of water, the strained juice and peel of 2 lemons, and a few drops of carmine (p. 71) in a pan, and let them just come to the boil. Pass it through the tammy and add 1 pint of custard (Nos. 1 to 4) or 1 pint of sweetened cream (No. 5), and 6 drops of lemon-juice. Partly freeze it, add half a pint of whipped cream, and finish as No. 10. Serve as a dessert ice.

16.—Brown Bread Ice (*Crème de Pain Bis*).

Make a pint of brown bread crumbs and mix them with 8 tablespoonfuls of noyeau or maraschino syrup (p. 70), a few drops of vanilla essence, and 1 pint of cream or unsweetened custard, and freeze dry. Serve in a pile or mould. This is a good entremet or dessert ice, and is much liked for garden and evening parties. It can also be served as a supper ice.

17.—Burnt Almond Cream Ice (*Crème de Pralines*).

Blanch and peel the almonds as in No. 10; put them in a sauté pan with an ounce of fresh butter and an ounce of castor sugar, and fry till a dark brown colour. Then pound in the mortar till smooth, adding by degrees 1 pint of hot milk or cream, in which 4 sheets of Marshall's gelatine have been dissolved, sweetened with three ounces of sugar, and 3 or 4 drops of essence of almonds. Pass it through the tammy or hair sieve. Freeze and finish as in No. 10. Serve as a dinner or dessert ice.

18.—Cedrat Cream Ice (*Crème à la Cédrat*).

Take one or two cedratti and rub them well with four or five large lumps of sugar, then add these lumps with the strained juice to a quart of lemon cream ice, and freeze. Serve rough or mould. Serve as a dessert or supper ice.

19.—Cherry Cream Ice (*Crème de Cerises*).

Stone 1 pound of cherries, break the stones, take out the kernels, and cook the cherries and kernels for about 10 minutes in half a pint of water and 3 ounces of castor sugar; then pound them, add the juice of $1\frac{1}{2}$ lemons, and a little carmine or cherry red to colour (p. 71). Pass it through a tammy cloth or hair sieve, add to a pint of custard (Nos. 1 to 4) or sweetened cream (No. 5) and a wine-glass of kirsch, and freeze. Serve in a pile on a napkin or mould it, and use as a dessert or supper ice.

20.—Chestnut Cream Ice (*Crème de Marrons*).

Roast a quart of chestnuts, and when fully softened remove all husk and skin and pound them in a mortar, adding during the pounding by degrees a few drops of essence of vanilla, 3 ounces of castor sugar, a pint of tepid cream, and 6 drops of carmine (p. 71). When well mixed pass it through hair sieve or tammy cloth. This may be frozen as it is, or added to a pint of custard (Nos. 1 to 4) or sweetened cream (No. 5), and finished as in previous recipes. Serve as a dinner or dessert ice.

21.—Chocolate Cream Ice (*Crème de Chocolat*).

Take a quarter of a pound of Fry's vanilla chocolate cut very fine, and put it in a stewpan with half a pint of milk or cold water on the stove to cook for about ten minutes; then add this to 1 pint of custard (Nos. 1 to 4) or 1 pint of sweetened cream (No. 5) and a few drops of vanilla essence. Freeze and finish as for vanilla cream ice (No. 58).

Cocoa cream ice may be made by adding 2 teaspoonfuls of soluble cocoa to 1 pint of custard, and finished as usual. Serve as a dinner or dessert ice.

22.—Cinnamon Cream Ice (*Crème de Cannelle*).

Put 1 pint of milk or cream to boil with a finger-length of cinnamon, 1 bayleaf, and the peel of half a lemon; when well flavoured, add 4 sheets of Marshall's gelatine, and mix it on to 8 raw yolks of eggs and 4 ounces of castor sugar; thicken over the fire. Add a little apricot yellow (p. 71); tammy, and finish as for other ices. Serve as a dessert ice.

23.—Cocoanut Cream Ice (*Crème de Noix de Coco*).

Grate a small cocoanut, and stir this with 1 quart of custard or cream just as you take the latter from the fire. Strain it through tammy or hair sieve, flavouring it with a quarter-pint of rose or orange-flower water. Freeze it and mould as before. Serve as a dinner, dessert, or supper ice.

24.—Coffee Cream Ice (*Crème de Café*).

Make 1 pint of strong coffee (or coffee extract is sometimes used), sweeten with 3 ounces of castor sugar ; add this to 1 quart of custard (p. 6). Freeze and finish as above. This ice will be brown, and not so delicate as the following. Serve as a dinner or dessert ice.

25.—White Coffee Cream Ice : very delicate (*Crème de Café blanche*).

Take a quarter of a pound of fresh roasted Mocha coffee berries, and add them to a pint of cream or milk in which dissolve 4 sheets of Marshall's gelatine ; let them stand on the stove in a bainmarie for an hour, but do not let them boil ; sweeten with 3 ounces of sugar ; strain through tammy. Freeze and finish as for vanilla cream ice (No. 58). Serve as a dinner or dessert ice.

26.—Cranberry Cream Ice (*Crème de Cranberges*).

Put 1 pound of cranberries in a pan with 6 ounces of castor sugar, a few drops of carmine (p. 71), and half a pint of water. Cook until a pulp, then pass it through the tammy, add 1 pint of sweetened cream (No. 5) or custard (Nos. 1 to 4), and half a wine-glass of maraschino syrup. Freeze and finish as for previous ices, and serve for dessert.

27.—Cucumber Cream Ice (*Crème de Concombres*).

Peel and remove the seeds from the cucumber, and to 1 large-sized cucumber add 4 ounces of castor sugar, the peel of two lemons, and ¾ of a pint of water; cook till tender. Then pound and add to it a wine-glass of ginger brandy, a little green colouring, and the juice of the two lemons; pass it through the tammy, and add to 1 pint of sweetened cream or custard. Freeze and finish as usual, and serve for dessert.

28.—Curaçoa Cream Ice (*Crème au Curaçoa*).

Take 1 pint of unsweetened custard (Nos. 1 to 4) or unsweetened cream; add the juice of 2 sweet oranges, 2 large wine-glasses of curaçoa or curaçoa syrup, 1½ ounces of castor sugar, a quarter-pint of orange-flower water and a few drops of vanilla essence. Freeze, and mould or serve roughly, for dinner or dessert ice.

29.—Damson Cream Ice (*Crème de Prunes de Damas*).

Put 1 pound of ripe damsons to cook with 6 ounces
of castor sugar, half a pint of water, the peel of
two oranges, four bayleaves, and a little liquid carmine; just boil up and then pass it through the
tammy; add the strained juice of the fruit. Add this
to 1 pint of custard or cream (Nos. 1 to 5), and half a
glass of noyeau syrup (p. 70), and freeze. Serve as a
dinner or dessert ice.

30.—Filbert Cream Ice (*Crème d'Avelines*).

Shell and put 1 pint of filberts in a pan with cold
water, and put to boil; when they boil strain off and
wash in cold water and rub them in a cloth to take
off the skins. When this is done, put the filberts in
the mortar and pound them till quite smooth; then
mix with them gently 8 raw yolks of eggs, 1 pint of
cream, 1 wine-glass of "Silver Rays" (white) rum, a
wine-glass of noyeau syrup, and 4 ounces of castor
sugar; put it into a pan and stir over the fire to
thicken, keeping it stirred all the time; then pass
through the tammy, add, when cold, a teaspoonful of
essence of vanilla and $\frac{1}{2}$ pint of whipped cream, and
freeze. Serve as a dinner or dessert ice.

31.—Ginger Cream Ice (*Crème au Gingembre*).

Pound half a pound of preserved ginger till smooth;
then add to it 10 raw yolks of eggs, 3 ounces of sugar,

1½ pints of cream, and 1 glass of ginger wine; thicken it over the fire, then tammy or rub it through a hair sieve, and freeze. Serve as a dinner or dessert ice.

32.—Gooseberry Cream Ice (*Crème de Groseilles Vertes*).

Put 1 quart of gooseberries on the stove in a pan, with half a pint of water, 6 ounces of castor sugar; boil, and when cooked pass through the tammy. If green berries, use a little sap green, or apple green (p. 71), to colour; if red, a little carmine or cherry red. When tammied, mix with a pint of sweetened cream or custard, and freeze. Serve for dessert.

33.—Greengage Cream Ice (*Crème de Prunes de Reine-Claude*).

Stone 2 pints of ripe greengages, put half a pint of water in a pan with 8 ounces of castor sugar and 4 sheets of Marshall's gelatine, and boil the fruit in this till quite smooth; then add a little green colouring, a wine-glassful of maraschino syrup, and pass through the tammy. Add this to 2 pints of custard or cream (Nos. 1 to 5), and finish as usual. Serve as a dinner or dessert ice.

34.—Italian Cream Ice (*Crème à l'Italienne*).

Scald 1½ pints of cream or milk, with a little lemon peel and cinnamon, and mix it on to 10 raw yolks of eggs, add 3 or 4 sheets of Marshall's gelatine; sweeten with 6 ounces of castor sugar; thicken over the fire, tammy, and flavour, when cool, with a large wine-glassful of pale brandy, half a glass of noyeau, the juice of 3 lemons, and a quarter-pint of rose-water. Freeze, and serve as in previous recipes, for dinner or dessert.

35.—Kirsch Cream Ice (*Crème au Kirsch*).

To 1½ pints of sweetened cream or custard add 3 wine-glasses of kirsch syrup, 1 glass of pale brandy, the juice of 3 oranges or lemons, and 3 or 4 drops of almond essence. Freeze. Serve as a dinner or dessert ice.

36.—Lemon Cream Ice (*Crème de Citron*).

Peel 6 lemons very thinly, and put this peel to boil, with 1¼ pints of cream or milk and 5 ounces of sugar, for 10 minutes; add 3 or 4 sheets of Marshall's gelatine; then mix on to 10 raw yolks of eggs, thicken it over the fire and pass through the tammy. When cool add the juice from the lemons, which must be strained, and freeze. Serve as a dinner or dessert ice. Any peel left can be chopped up and used for flavouring puddings, cakes, etc.

37.—Marmalade, Orange or Lemon, Cream Ice (*Crème au Marmelade*).

Mix 4 tablespoonfuls of marmalade with 1 pint of cream or unsweetened custard and the juice of 2 of

the fruit, either lemon or orange, and 1 wine-glassful
of orange or lemon syrup. Pass it through the
tammy or hair sieve, and freeze. Serve as a dinner
or dessert ice.

38.—Maraschino Cream Ice (*Crème au Marasquin*).

To 1 pint of cream or unsweetened custard add 4
wine-glasses of maraschino or maraschino syrup and
the strained juice of 2 lemons and 1 orange, and
freeze. Serve for dinners or suppers.

39.—Neapolitan or Pinachée Cream Ices (*Petites Crèmes à la Napolitaine*).

You must have a Neapolitan box for this ice (p.
59), and fill it up in 3 or 4 layers with different
coloured and flavoured ice creams (a water ice may
be used with the custards); for instance, lemon,
vanilla, chocolate, and pistachio. Freeze it in the
patent ice cave for about 2½ to 3 hours, then dip the
box into cold water for a second or two, turn out
the ice, cut it into slices crosswise about ¼ inch thick,
put each into a Neapolitan paper, and arrange neatly
on a dish on a napkin or dish paper.

These ices can be arranged on a border of ice-
water, when they should be prepared as follows:
Take the oblong fancy border mould, fill it with cold
water, put on the lid, and place it in the charged cave

for 2½ to 3 hours, then dip it into cold water, turn out the border on to a flat or dessert dish with a fancy paper, on which put a thin strip of wadding; arrange the Neapolitan ices in their papers on the border so that the various colours show up well; place on the ice a little sprig of maidenhair or asparagus fern; and use for a dinner or dessert ice, or for afternoon teas, tennis-parties, etc.

40.—Noyeau Cream Ice (*Crème au Noyeau*).

To 1 pint of cream add 2 glasses of noyeau liqueur or 4 tablespoonfuls of noyeau syrup, and the juice of 2 oranges and 1 lemon. Freeze. Serve as a dinner or dessert ice.

41.—Orange Cream Ice (*Crème à l'Orange*).

This is made as for lemon (No. 36), using oranges instead of lemons. Serve as a dinner or dessert ice. The peels can be chopped up and used for flavouring puddings, cakes, etc.

42.—Orange Flower Water Cream Ice (*Crème à la Fleur d'Oranger*).

Blanch and skin 4 ounces of sweet almonds and 6 whole bitter almonds; pound them in the mortar till quite smooth, then mix with a quarter of a pint of cream, 6 ounces of castor sugar, and 7 raw yolks of eggs; add, when this is mixed well, 1¼ pints of

cream, and then thicken over the fire, and tammy.
When cool, add two wine-glasses of orange-flower
water, a few drops of essence of vanilla, half a wine-
glass of "Silver Rays" (white) rum, and freeze it.
Serve as a dinner, dessert, or ball supper ice.

43.—Peach Cream Ice (*Crème de Pêches*).

This is made in the same manner as the apricot
ice. A *very* little carmine and apricot yellow is used
for the colour. Serve for dinner or dessert.

44.—Pear Cream Ice (*Crème de Poires*).

This is made in the same manner as the apple ice
(No. 11), colouring with sap green or carmine, or it
may be left plain. It can be served as a dinner or
dessert ice.

45.—Pine-apple Cream Ice (*Crème d'Ananas*).

Peel off the outside of the pine-apple; if not fully
ripe, it will require to be boiled for about 20 minutes.
Put the pine-apple in a clean pan with 1½ to 2 pints of
water and half a pound of sugar, and cook till tender.
Then pound, and pass through hair sieve or tammy.
To half a pint of this purée add 1 pint of cream or
custard (Nos. 1 to 5). Freeze. Colour the ice
required for the body of the pine-apple mould with
apricot yellow, and that for the top with a little apple
green. Another way is to make a purée of the tinned

pine-apple, and add it to the custard or cream (Nos. 1
to 5). See coloured plate. Serve as a dinner or
dessert ice.

46.—Pistachio Cream Ice (*Crème de Pistaches*).

Blanch, peel, and pound a quarter of a pound of
pistachio kernels. Add, when thoroughly pounded,
2 tablespoonfuls of orange-flower water, and 12 drops
vanilla essence; pass through sieve or tammy, and
add 1 pint of sweetened cream or custard (Nos. 1
to 4). Colour with apple green or sap green (p. 71).
Freeze and mould. Serve for a dinner or dessert ice.

47.—Plum Cream Ice (*Crème de Prunes*).

Put 2 pounds of plums in a pan with half a pint
of water, half a pound of castor sugar, a few drops
of carmine, and the purée of 2 lemons; cook till
smooth, and pass through the tammy. To half a pint
of this purée add 1 pint of slightly sweetened cream
or custard (Nos. 1 to 5). A few drops of essence
of almonds and the strained juice of the lemons will
improve it. Freeze and mould or serve in a pile, and
use for a dinner or dessert ice.

48.—Quince Cream Ice (*Crème de Coings*).

Take 4 tablespoonfuls of quince jam, and add to it
the juice of 2 oranges and of half a lemon, 1½ pints of
cream or custard (unsweetened), a little apricot yellow
to colour, 2 tablespoonfuls of pine-apple syrup, a few

drops of vanilla essence, and half a wine-glass of "Silver Rays" (white) rum. Pass it through the tammy and freeze it.

49.—Raspberry Cream Ice (*Crème de Framboises*).

Take 1 pound of raspberries, 6 ounces of castor sugar, and the juice of a lemon; mix with one good pint of custard or cream (Nos. 1 to 5). Tammy, and colour with liquid carmine or cherry red (p. 71). Freeze, and finish as for other ices. Serve as a dinner or dessert ice.

50.—Ratafia Cream Ice (*Crème au Ratafia*).

Bruise 1 pound of ratafia biscuits in the mortar. Make a custard (see Nos. 1 to 4) of 1½ pints of milk, 10 raw yolks of eggs, and 6 ounces of castor sugar; and when it thickens, pour it over the bruised biscuits, and pass altogether through the tammy or hair sieve. Add half a wine-glass of noyeau syrup, and freeze. The crumbs may be left in the custard if liked. Serve for dinner or dessert.

51.—Red Currant Cream Ice (*Crème de Groseilles*).

Make this as for raspberry cream ice (No. 49), and serve for dessert, etc.

52.—Rhubarb Cream Ice (*Crème de Rhubarbe*).

Make this as for gooseberry cream ice (No. 32), using good ripe rhubarb; colour with Marshall's carmine, and use for suppers, tennis parties, etc.

53.—Rice Cream Ice (*Crème de Riz*).

Put 2 pints of new milk or cream to boil with 8 ounces of castor sugar, the peel of a lemon, 3 bay leaves, and a little crushed stick cinnamon, about 1 inch long; add 2 or 3 sheets of Marshall's gelatine, then put 3 ounces of rice cream (*crème de riz*) in a basin, and mix it into a smooth paste with cold milk, add the boiled milk, and let the whole simmer for 10 minutes. Pass it through the tammy, strainer, or sieve, and when cold add a few drops of essence of vanilla, and freeze. During the freezing add half a pint of slightly sweetened whipped cream that is slightly flavoured with vanilla essence. Mould or serve roughly, for dinner or dessert.

54.—Spanish Nut Cream Ice (*Crème de Noisettes*).

Break a pint of Spanish nuts and bake the kernels till crisp, then pound them till smooth, and add the raw yolks of 8 eggs, 5 ounces of castor sugar, and 1 pint of cream; put in a stew-pan and stir over the fire till it thickens, then pass it through the tammy cloth. When cool, add a wine-glass of noyeau syrup, half a wine-glass of brandy, half a pint of stiffly whipped cream, and 2 stiffly whipped whites of eggs. Freeze and mould or serve in glasses, for a dinner or dessert ice.

Spanish Nut Cream Ice. Another way.

Put the kernels of a pint of Spanish nuts, with 2 ounces of castor sugar, the finely chopped peel of 2 oranges and a tablespoonful of orange-flower water, in a sauté or stew-pan, and toss over a quick fire until the kernels are quite brown; then pound in the mortar, and mix well with half a pint of cream, pass through tammy cloth or hair sieve; flavour with 2 tablespoonfuls of maraschino or noyeau syrup (p. 70). Add this to 1 pint of the sweetened custard or cream (Nos. 1 to 5) and 2 tablespoonfuls of sherry. Freeze and mould or serve rough, for dinner, etc.

55.—Strawberry Cream Ice (*Crème de Fraises*).

Make this as raspberry cream (No. 49), and serve for a dinner ice.

56.—Tangarine Cream Ice (*Crème de Tangarines*).

Peel 12 tangarine oranges; make a pulp of the insides, first removing the pips. Put the peels in a pint of boiling cream or milk, and let it stand on the stove for a quarter of an hour, in a bainmarie with boiling water round it, but do not let it boil; add 4 sheets of Marshall's gelatine, then mix this with 8 raw yolks of eggs and 4 ounces of sugar, and stir over the fire till it thickens; now add the orange pulp, colour with apricot yellow, and pass through the tammy or hair sieve; when cool, add a wine-glass of orange-flower water, and freeze. This may be added to 1 pint of sweetened cream or custard (Nos. 1 to 5) before freezing. Use for dinner, etc.

57.—Tea Cream Ice (*Crème de Thé*).

Prepare half a pint of very strong tea, sweetened with 2 ounces of castor sugar, and add this to 1 pint of sweetened custard or cream Nos. (1 to 5), and finish as for other ices. Use for teas, dessert, suppers, etc.

58.—Vanilla Cream Ice (*Crème de Vanille*).

Prepare a custard (Nos. 1 to 4) or take sweetened cream (No. 5) and flavour with vanilla essence. Freeze and mould or serve in glasses, for ball suppers, dessert, etc. This is much improved by adding, during the freezing, a quarter of a pint of whipped cream to each pint of cream or custard.

To flavour with vanilla pods cut them in strips, and let them boil with the milk or cream of your custard, keeping the pan covered. The pods can be used twice or thrice for flavouring milk, etc., and then, if they are pounded whilst quite dry with a little castor sugar and then rubbed through a hair sieve, the powder can be used for other purposes.

59.—Walnut Cream Ice (*Crème de Noix*).

Make this as for filbert cream ice (No. 30), and serve for dessert.

60.—White Wine Cream Ice (*Crème au Vin blanc*).

Prepare a custard (No. 1) with 10 raw yolks of eggs, 1 pint of cream, and 4 ounces of sugar. When cool, add 3 glasses of white wine, 1 ditto pine-apple syrup, and freeze. When frozen, mix in 6 ounces of finely cut preserved fruits of any kind you have, and mould if desired. Serve for dessert, etc.

FRUIT SYRUPS.

N.B.—If the prepared syrups referred to in some of the foregoing recipes cannot be got at the time required, recourse may be had to the syrup in recipe No. 87 for sweetening purposes.

WATER ICES.

61.—Water Ices made from Jams.

To 4 tablespoonfuls of jam add 1 pint of cold water, the juice of 1 lemon; colour according to the fruit; pass through the tammy, and freeze. See note to No. 6.

62.—Water Ices made from Fruit Syrups.

To half a pint of water add 4 tablespoonfuls of the syrup (p. 70). Colour according to the fruit, and freeze. See note to No. 8.

WATER AND PERFUMED ICES MADE FROM RIPE FRUITS, ETC.

63.—Apple Ice Water (*Eau de Pommes*).

Put 1 pound of apples to cook in a pint of water, with a little lemon-peel, cinnamon, the juice of 1 lemon and 4 ounces of sugar, add 4 sheets of Marshall's gelatine; when cooked, pass through the tammy, and add to 1 pint of the purée 1 pint of water sweetened with 4 ounces of sugar or 8 tablespoonfuls of syrup (No. 87). Freeze and serve moulded or roughly.

64.—Apricot Ice Water (*Eau d'Abricots*).

Take 12 apricots and stone them, break the stones and pound the kernels; put the apricots to cook in a clean pan with 6 ounces of sugar, 1 pint of water, and cook them till quite smooth with 4 sheets of Marshall's gelatine; add a little apricot yellow, pass through the tammy, and add 1 pint of this pulp to 1 pint of water sweetened with sugar as in No. 63, or use the syrup No. 87, 8 tablespoonfuls to the pint of water, and freeze. Use for dessert, tennis parties, garden parties, etc.

65.—Banana Ice Water (*Eau de Bananes*).

Peel 6 ripe bananas, pound them, and add 4 ounces of sugar, 1½ pints of water, and the juice of 2 oranges or a quarter-pint of orange-flower water, or lemons if preferred, a little banana essence if you have it ; pass through tammy, and freeze.   Serve for dessert, etc.

66.—Bergamot Ice Water (*Eau de Bergamote*).

Prepare a lemon or orange ice water for this, and to 1½ pints of it add 2 wine-glasses of pale brandy and 6 drops of essence of bergamot.   Freeze dry, and serve for dessert, suppers, etc.

67.—Black Currant Ice Water (*Eau de Cassis*).

This is made in the same manner as the cranberry ice water, and can be used for tennis parties, dessert, etc.

68.—Cedrat Ice Water (*Eau de Cédrat*).

Prepare 1 quart lemon ice water (No. 75), rub off the zest of two fine cedratti with a piece of loaf sugar, add to it the lemon water, tammy or strain it, and freeze.   A quarter-pint of strained orange juice with 6 or 8 drops of vanilla essence is a great improvement. Serve for ball suppers or dessert.

69.—Cherry Ice Water (*Eau de Cerises*).

Stone 2 pounds of Kentish cherries, crack the stones and pound the kernels, pour 1 quart of boiling water on the fruit and kernels and half a pound of sugar, add 4 sheets of Marshall's gelatine ; colour with carmine and let stand till cold, then pass through the tammy, add a wine-glassful of kirsch, and, if liked, a wine-glassful of " Silver Rays " (white) rum or brandy, and freeze.

70.—Cranberry Ice Water (*Eau de Cranberges*).

Put half a pound of cranberries to cook with 8 ounces of sugar, the peel of 2 oranges and of 2 lemons, and half a pint of water; when cooked, add the juice of 2 lemons and 2 oranges, also dissolve in it 2 or 3 sheets of Marshall's gelatine, a little carmine, and pass through the tammy. Add half a pint of this pulp to 1 pint of water slightly sweetened, and freeze.

71.—Damson Ice Water (*Eau de Prunes de Damas*).

Stone 1 quart of damsons and make in the same manner as cherry ice water (No. 69). Freeze either for fancy moulds or to serve rough.

72.—Ginger Ice Water (*Eau de Gingembre*).

Pound 8 ounces of preserved ginger, mix it with 1 quart of orange ice water (No. 79); pass it through the tammy, and freeze. Either mould or serve rough.

73.—Grape Ice Water (*Eau de Raisin*).

To 1 pint of lemon ice water (No. 75) add a large wine-glassful of elder-flower water and 2 wine-glassfuls of sherry Freeze, and mould or serve rough. This will be greatly improved by the addition of a wine-glass of " Silver Rays " rum.

74.—Jasmine Ice Water (*Eau de Jasmin*).

This is made in the same way as bergamot, only essence of jasmine is used instead of bergamot. Freeze for moulding or to serve rough. This is very good served with meringues arranged with whipped cream flavoured with vanilla and sweetened.

75.—Lemon Ice Water (*Eau de Citron*).

1 pint of boiling water poured on to the peel of 8 lemons, half a pound of loaf sugar, and 4 sheets of Marshall's gelatine; when cool, mix with the juice of 6 lemons; add 6 drops of lemon essence; tammy or strain through sieve, and freeze for moulding or for serving in glasses.

76.—Mille Fruits Ice Water (*Eau de Mille Fruits*).

Prepare 1 quart of lemon ice ; add to it when partly frozen half a pound of mixed fruits cut in square pieces; any kind of fruit left from dessert will do for this ice. Serve in mould or rough.

77.—Melon Ice Water (*Eau de Melon*).

Take off the skin from a ripe melon about 1½ lbs. in weight, and pound the melon till smooth, then add half a pint of boiling water in which 4 sheets of Marshall's gelatine has been dissolved, 3 ounces of sugar, the juice of 2 oranges or lemons, 1 wine-glass of curaçoa or maraschino syrup, 1 wine-glass of "Silver Rays" (white) rum, and ¾ ounce of ground ginger; add this to 1 pint of water, and freeze for moulding or to serve rough.

78.—Mulberry Ice Water (*Eau de Mûres*).

Pick and then pound 1 pound of mulberries; add to them 4 ounces of sugar, a little liquid carmine, juice of 1 lemon; the addition of 2 wine-glasses of port is an improvement; pass through the tammy, then add to 1 pint of cold water, and freeze. Serve as in previous recipes for dessert, tennis parties, etc.

79.—Orange Ice Water (*Eau d'Oranges*).

Prepare this the same as for lemon ice water, only use oranges instead of lemons, and serve for ball suppers, dessert, etc.

80.—Peach Ice Water (*Eau de Pêches*).

Peel 6 good ripe peaches, crack the stones, and remove the kernels, which must be pounded; put in a stew-pan with 1 pint of water, 4 ounces of sugar, and juice and peel of 2 lemons; cook the fruit for 15 minutes, pound it up smoothly, then tammy, and add a wine-glassful of noyeau, 1 glass of orange-flower water and the strained juice of two oranges, and a little carmine. Freeze, and use for ball suppers, dessert, etc.

81.—Pear Ice Water (*Eau de Poires*).

Peel and core 6 good-sized mellow pears, cut them in slices, and put them to cook in 1½ pints of water with 6 ounces of sugar, the peel of 2 lemons, a pounded split vanilla pod 1 inch long, and a little cinnamon; add a little carmine and, when cooked, mix with a pint of lemon ice water; pass them through a tammy, and freeze.

82.—Pine-apple Ice Water (*Eau d'Ananas*).

Peel the pine and take out the cores, put it to cook for 15 minutes, with 1½ pints of water, 6 ounces of sugar, and the juice of 2 lemons and 2 oranges, strain off the juice, pound the fruit; mix the liquor in which it was cooked with it and pass through the tammy or hair sieve, and freeze. A few pieces of the pine-apple may be cut in rounds or dice shapes, and added to the frozen ice just before serving. Mould if wished, and use for dessert, etc.

83.—Raspberry Ice Water (*Eau de Framboises*).

This is prepared the same as for strawberry ice water, only using raspberries instead of strawberries. Serve for dinners, suppers, etc.

84.—Red Currant Ice Water (*Eau de Groseilles*).

Proceed as for black currant ice water, only use red currants instead of black. Freeze, and mould if wished, and serve for dessert, ball suppers, tennis parties, etc.

85.—Rose Water Ice (*Eau de Roses*).

Take half a pound of fresh-gathered rose leaves, pour 1 pint of boiling water on them, with 4 ounces of sugar, and keep closely covered up; then strain off and colour with a little liquid carmine, $\frac{1}{2}$ pint of rose water and a teaspoonful of vanilla essence, and freeze. Use for ball suppers, dessert, tennis parties, etc.

86.—Strawberry Ice Water (*Eau de Fraises*).

Put the strawberries in the mortar and pound them, and to 1 pound add 6 ounces of castor sugar, the juice of 1 lemon, a little liquid carmine; pass though the tammy or hair sieve, mix this to 1 pint of cold water, and freeze. Serve as in previous recipes for ball suppers, dessert, tennis-parties, etc.

87.—Syrup for Water Ices.

Put $1\frac{1}{2}$ pounds of loaf sugar in a clean pan to boil with 3 pints of cold water, keep well skimmed, reduce to half the quantity, and strain through the tammy or clean cloth. This will keep well. It may be used

for sweetening the ices instead of the sugar, and if
4 sheets of Marshall's gelatine are dissolved in each
pint of the water, it greatly improves the ice-making,
and creates a much smoother creamy ice.

SORBETS, ETC.

The Italian word *sorbetto*, meaning sherbet, shows the origin of
these dishes. Their general character is that of a water ice mixed or
flavoured with wine or spirits. They are served before the roast in
glasses or fancy cups, and generally just enough frozen to be piled up
in the glass, or they may be moulded in little shapes and served with
or without fruit. The following recipes will be sufficient for guidance,
and they can be varied according to desire.

88.—Sorbet of Peaches (*Sorbet de Pêches à la Portugaise*).

Take 6 ripe peaches, peel them, and add to
them 6 ounces of castor sugar, the juice of 2 oranges
or 1 dozen grapes; crack the stones, pound the
kernels and put to the fruit, and add to 1 pint of cold
water, in which 4 sheets of Marshall's gelatine has been
dissolved; add about 6 drops of Marshall's carmine
and half a saltspoonful of apricot yellow, and tammy;
then freeze, and when frozen add 1 wine-glassful of
kirsch, a wine-glass of "Silver Rays" (white) rum,
and serve with sliced fresh peaches, that have been
sprinkled with any nice liqueur and then left on
ice till quite cold but not frozen, and chopped pistachio nuts over, for dinner, dessert, tennis, etc.

89.—Sorbet of Strawberries (*Sorbet de Fraises*).

Take 1 pound of strawberries, and add to them
8 ounces of castor sugar, a little carmine, and the juice
of 1 lemon; pass through the tammy, and to this add
1 pint of water, in which 3 or 4 sheets of Marshall's
gelatine has been dissolved, and partly freeze; then
add 1 wine-glassful of curaçoa (p. 70), half a wine-
glassful of " Silver Rays " rum; continue the freezing,
and serve in sorbet cups or glasses. If you have little
strawberry moulds, you can put the sorbet in them,
and freeze them for about half an hour in the cave.
Serve with cut fresh fruits over, which have been
flavoured by being tossed in a little brandy and
castor sugar.

90.—Sorbet of Apricots (*Sorbet d'Abricots à la Moscovite*).

Take 4 tablespoonfuls of apricot jam, about a saltspoonful of apricot yellow, 1 pint of cold water, pass
through the tammy and freeze; then add 1 wine-
glassful of maraschino (p. 70) and half a wine-glassful
of " Silver Rays " rum; freeze firm, and serve on
a dish on a paper or napkin with square pieces of
apricots, cherries, and angelica that have been
sprinkled over with a little maraschino syrup. In
summer-time fresh fruit can be used, when the fruit
should be cut up and a little sugar sprinkled over it
before serving. This is served in sorbet cups or glasses
or in a coupe shape.

91.—Roman Punch (*Punch à la Romaine*).

Boil 1 quart of water, and add to it 1 pound of sugar; when quite boiling, pour it on to the peel of 6 lemons, add ¼ ounce of Marshall's gelatine, cover it over till cold, then add the juice of 6 lemons; strain it through the tammy, and freeze; when partly frozen, add 2 wine-glasses of "Silver Rays" (white) rum, and serve in sorbet cups or in glasses, or in a coupe shape, standing it on a serviette, for dinner, ball supper, etc.

92.—Another way.

Make 1 quart of lemon ice water in which ¼ ounce of Marshall's gelatine has been dissolved; when cold, have the whites of 5 eggs whipped stiff, with a tiny pinch of salt, then mixed with 4 ounces of castor sugar; partly freeze the lemon ice, and then mix to it the whipped egg, and continue freezing in the machine till smooth; when smooth, add 1 large wine-glassful of brandy and a half-pint of champagne; freeze it to the proper consistency, and serve in sorbet cups or glasses, or in a coupe shape, and serve for dinner, ball supper, etc.

93.—American Sorbet (*Sorbet à l'Américaine*).

Make some imitation glasses, by freezing water in the proper tin moulds prepared for the purpose, and make a sorbet as above, flavouring it with Catawba wine or champagne. Serve the sorbet in the imitation

D

glasses. These imitation cups or glasses can be made transparent, marble-like, or coloured. Use for any cold collation or for dinner.

94.—Rum Sorbet (*Sorbet au Rhum*).

Prepare a lemon water ice, and when nearly frozen, flavour with 2 wine-glasses of "Silver Rays" rum to the pint of prepared ice, refreeze it to proper consistency and serve for dinner or any cold service.

MOUSSES.

These make excellent sweets, and are very much liked on account of their lightness. They are served as an entremet, sometimes for dessert. The following recipes will show the method of making them.

Mousses are greatly improved in appearance if, after they are turned out of the moulds, they are replaced in the charged ice cave, on a little tray or dish, and allowed to remain for 20 to 30 minutes before being used.

95.—Coffee Mousse (*Mousse au Café*).

Put into a stew-pan 4 raw yolks of eggs, 2 whites, 1 ounce of castor sugar, 1 large tablespoonful of strong coffee, or ½ tablespoonful of coffee essence, and a saltspoonful of vanilla essence; whip over boiling water or over a fire till it is warm, then take off and whip till cold and like a stiff batter, and then add half a pint of stiffly whipped and slightly sweetened cream; mix these together, being careful not to overstir, after the cream is added, or it will be liable to curdle. Put in a plain bomb or other mould, and place in the charged ice cave to freeze for about 3½ hours. To turn out, dip the mould in cold water, pass a clean cloth over the bottom to absorb any moisture. Serve with dish-paper, or napkin on dish, for dinner or dessert.

96.—Strawberry Mousse (*Mousse aux Fraises*).

Put 4 raw yolks of eggs into a pan, with 2 whites of eggs, 2 ounces of castor sugar, a quarter of a pint of the pulp of fresh strawberries, 1 teaspoonful of essence of vanilla, a little of liquid carmine to colour; whip till warm over boiling water, as in previous recipe, then remove and whip till cold and thick, and add half a pint of lightly sweetened whipped cream; mix carefully together, put into any fancy mould, and freeze for about 3½ to 4 hours in the cave. Turn out and dish same as No. 95. When fresh fruits are not obtainable, 2 tablespoonfuls of strawberry syrup with a few drops of lemon juice can be used instead.

97.—Maraschino Mousse (*Mousse au Marasquin*).

This is made in the same manner as the Mousse à la Vanille, but instead of the vanilla essence add 1 good wine-glassful of maraschino for flavour, and use for dinner or dessert.

98.—Vanilla Mousse (*Mousse à la Vanille*).

Put 6 yolks of eggs into a whipping-pan, with 2 whites, 1 ounce of castor sugar, half a table-spoonful of essence of vanilla, and a tablespoonful of brandy; whip this over boiling water till warm, then remove the pan from the fire and continue whipping till cold and thick, then add to this half a pint of slightly sweetened whipped cream; put into any kind of mould, and set in the ice cave for $3\frac{1}{2}$ to 4 hours. Turn out same as No. 95.

ICED SOUFFLÉS.

These very much resemble the Mousses, but as they are served in dishes or cases, and the mousses are moulded, a slight difference is required in the ingredients and in the time for freezing. The following recipes will be sufficient for guidance.

99.—Coffee Soufflé (*Soufflé au Café*).

Take a soufflé dish or paper soufflé case and surround it outside with paper standing about 2 to 3 inches above the top, and if a dish is used put it into the charged cave to get cold.

Put into a whipping tin and whip over boiling water 2 raw yolks of eggs, 2 whole, 1 large tablespoonful of very strong coffee, 1 ounce of castor sugar, until like a thick batter, then remove and continue the whipping till the mixture is cold; to this quantity add $\frac{1}{4}$ pint of slightly sweetened whipped cream; pour this into the case, letting it rise above the case to near the top of the paper. Freeze in the cave for $3\frac{1}{2}$ to 4 hours, and serve in the case with a folded napkin round or a fancy paper band; place the soufflé on a flat dish on a paper, and serve for dinner

or dessert. Of course these quantities may be pro-
portionately increased or diminished to suit the size
of the dish or case.

100.—Vanilla Soufflé (*Soufflé à la Vanille*).

Prepare the soufflé dish or paper case as in No. 99.
Put into a whipping-tin 4 raw yolks of eggs, 2
whites, 1 ounce of castor sugar, a saltspoonful of
vanilla essence, and a dessert-spoonful of brandy;
whip over boiling water until warm, then remove it
and whip it cold and like a thick batter; then add
about ¼ pint of lightly · sweetened whipped cream.
Finish as in No. 99, and serve for dinner or dessert.

101.—Strawberry Soufflé (*Soufflé de Fraises*).

Prepare a mousse as in No. 96, using about half as
much more cream whipped, finish as in last recipe,
and serve for dinner or dessert.

102.—Coffee Soufflés in Cases (*Petits Soufflés au Café*).

Take the little paper soufflé cases and fasten round
the outside of each a strip of white foolscap paper,
about 3 inches deep, fixing it with sealing wax; let
the paper stand about 1½ inches above the top of the
case. Prepare some of the soufflé mixture as in
No. 99; fill the cases to nearly the edge of the paper
surrounding them, and place them in the charged cave
for 2½ to 3 hours; when frozen sufficiently remove the

papers and slip each case into a little fancy paper
case, and serve on a flat dish on a fancy paper, for
dinner, or dessert, or any cold collation.

Any soufflé can be served in a similar manner.
Fruit and vanilla soufflés would be improved in
appearance by sprinkling a little coloured sugar over
them, or a little finely chopped pistachio. They are
also pretty when garnished on the top with a little
rose shape of sweetened, flavoured, and mottled cream,
forced through a forcing-bag and large rose pipe.
They may also be garnished with raw or ripe fruits
which have been glazed with boiled sugar.

DRESSED ICES, ETC.

It is impossible to give more than a few under this head, as the
variety that can be made with the various moulds, flavours, etc., is
almost unlimited; but the mixtures which can be used will be found
among the foregoing recipes, and some designs in colours are given in
the book as examples, also a list of some moulds on pages 53 to 62.

103.—Strawberry and Vanilla Bombe (*Bombe à la Vanille et Fraises*).

Prepare 1 pint of strawberry ice water and freeze
it quite dry, have three-quarters of a pint of vanilla
custard prepared with three-quarters of a pint of
milk or cream boiled with a stick of vanilla pod, 2
ounces of castor sugar, 2 sheets of Marshall's gelatine,
and when flavoured sufficiently pour on to 4 raw
yolks of eggs and thicken over the fire; then tammy

and freeze, and add, when partly frozen, 3 tablespoonfuls of maraschino syrup and 6 drops of brandy; line a bombe mould with the strawberry water ice, and fill up the centre with the vanilla custard, and freeze for 3½ to 4 hours in the charged patent ice cave. To turn out, dip the mould in cold water, pass a clean cloth over the bottom to absorb any moisture, and serve on a napkin or fancy paper on a flat dish or plate, for a dinner ice.

104.—Bombe with Fruits (*Bombe aux Fruits*).

Take a bombe mould, which should be stood in a basin or tin with a mixture of ice and salt all round it, and line it with chocolate ice cream, then fill up the centre with vanilla cream ice mixed with a wineglassful of kirsch, half a pint of whipped cream, and a quarter of a pound of candied fruits cut in small dice pieces which have been soaked in a tablespoonful of noyeau syrup. Freeze in charged ice cave for 4 hours, turn out as in last recipe, and serve on a dishpaper or napkin.

105.—Sovereign Bombe (*Bombe à la Souveraine*).

Line the sides and top of a bomb-shaped mould with a layer of almond ice cream, and fill up the interior with a tea mousse (see recipe No. 95 for coffee mousse).

Freeze in the cave for 3 to 4 hours according to size of mould; when ready to use turn out the ice in the usual way, and serve it on a border of sponge cake, and garnish the dish with the same cake cut in small fancy shapes.

106.—Plain Ice Pudding (*Pouding Glacé*).

To 1½ pints of good cream add half a pint of new milk ; put it in a stew-pan with the raw yolks of 12 eggs, a pinch of mixed spice, half a pound of castor sugar, 1 split pod of vanilla; stir this over the fire till it thickens and presents a creamy appearance on the wooden spoon, then add 4 sheets of Marshall's gelatine; tammy it, and when cool add a large wine-glassful of brandy or "Silver Rays" rum, a wine-glassful of kirsch, 4 ounces of dried mixed fruits cut up into dice shapes, and half a pint of slightly sweetened whipped cream; freeze, and put into any mould and freeze in the cave for 2 hours.   Serve for dinner or dessert.

107.—Nesselrode Pudding (*Pouding à la Nesselrode*).

This is prepared the same as No. 106, with the addition of various cut fruits, and 1 ounce of shelled blanched Jordan almonds cut into dice shapes and baked brown, being mixed with the custard before putting into the mould.   If fresh or dried fruits are used, they should be soaked in a little liqueur or spirit and sprinkled with sugar before being mixed. Fruits preserved in syrups may simply be cut up and mixed.

108.—Sauce for above.

A sauce is sometimes served with the Nesselrode pudding, and is made by preparing a thick rich custard (No. 1) and flavouring it with vanilla or maraschino. Keep it on the ice, and serve as cold as possible.

109.—Chateaubriand Bombe (*Bombe à la Chateaubriand*).

Prepare 2 pints of vanilla custard (Nos. 1 to 4), put the milk to boil with $4\frac{1}{2}$ ounces of castor sugar and 1 pod of vanilla split in shreds; let this come to the boil, and remain on the side of the stove in a bainmarie pan covered up for about 15 minutes, but it must not boil; add 4 sheets of Marshall's gelatine, then mix it on to 12 raw yolks of eggs and thicken over the fire. Divide the custard into two parts; put to one part a few drops of essence of vanilla and $\frac{1}{4}$ pint of orange-flower water, and colour it with apple green to the colour of pistachio, and tammy; it is ready then to freeze, but when partly frozen put about $\frac{1}{2}$ pint of whipped cream, sweetened with half a teaspoonful of castor sugar. Put 3 ounces of blanched sweet almonds in a sauté pan, with half an ounce of fresh butter and 1 ounce of castor sugar; make these quite a deep brown over the fire, and then pound them quickly in the mortar till smooth; mix them with the other part of vanilla custard, and pass through the tammy; when frozen, add cream as to the other part of the custard, and freeze. Arrange the two ices thus prepared in a fancy mould in layers, or the mould can be entirely lined with the green, and the centre filled with the brown ice. Freeze for 2 hours in the cave, and serve for a dinner or dessert ice.

110.—Ginger Bombe (*Bombe au Gingembre*).

Prepare a custard made with a pint of milk, boiled with the peel of 2 lemons and 3 ounces of castor sugar; when the milk boils, mix it on to 4 raw yolks of eggs and as much ginger as will cover a threepenny piece, thicken over the fire and tammy, then add the strained juice of the lemons and 6 drops of vanilla essence, and when cool freeze; when partly frozen, add half a pint of whipped cream sweetened with half an ounce of castor sugar; line the bombe mould with this, forming a well, and have 3 ounces of preserved ginger cut in dice shapes and flavoured with a little maraschino and put in the centre; fill up with more of the custard, and freeze for $3\frac{1}{2}$ hours in the cave. Turn out in the usual way and serve on a napkin or dish-paper, for dinner or dessert.

111.—Bartlett Pudding (*Pouding à la Bartlett*).

Peel and cut up in thin slices 6 ripe Bartlett pears, cook them in $1\frac{1}{2}$ pints of water with the juice of 2 lemons, 6 ounces of sugar; when tender, add 3 or 4 sheets of Marshall's gelatine, drain them on a sieve, and pass the fruit through a tammy or fine hair sieve; mix with this 2 ounces of pine-apple cut fine, 2 ounces of dried cherries, and a pint of thick cream, and freeze; when partly frozen, have ready to mix with it the whipped whites of 3 eggs, to which have been added 2 ounces of sugar, cooked to caramel. For this, put the sugar to boil with a quarter of a pint of water, and when cooked add 2 ounces more of water, and when boiled up and liquid mix it with the eggs and add to the frozen mixture, and continue the freezing, and mould. Put it to freeze in the charged ice cave for 3½ to 4 hours, then turn out as usual. A little of the syrup from the pears must be used for the sauce for serving round the pudding. Prepare it as follows: Whip the white of 1 egg and mix it with 2 tablespoonfuls of whipped cream, half a wine-glass of maraschino syrup (p. 70); add a wine-glassful of the pear syrup and cool on ice. When the pudding is turned out, pour the sauce over it, and serve for a dinner sweet.

112.—Plombière of Strawberries (*Plombière de Fraises*).

Put 1 pint of thick cream in a pan with the raw yolks of 12 eggs, a tiny pinch of mixed spice, and half a pound of castor sugar; stir together on the stove, and when nearly boiling add to it 4 sheets of Marshall's gelatine, 1 pint of the pulp of fresh strawberries which has been passed through the tammy cloth, a little carmine, half a teaspoonful of essence of vanilla, a wine-glass of brandy, 3 whipped whites of eggs, and half a pint of whipped cream; freeze and mould, and leave in the ice cave for 4 hours; then dip in cold water, and turn out on to a napkin or dish-paper.

113.—Muscovite of Oranges (*Moscovite d'Oranges*).

Put half a pound of loaf sugar with the peel of 8 or 10 oranges, a quarter of an ounce of Marshall's gelatine, and pour over them 1 pint of boiling water and a little saffron yellow; let this stand till cool, then mix the juice of the oranges to it and strain through the tammy, add a wine-glass of maraschino and brandy to flavour. Pour into a mould and freeze for about 4 hours in the charged ice cave; turn out as in the last recipe. This can be served with whipped cream sweetened and flavoured, which should be arranged in the form of a rose by means of a forcing-bag and large rose pipe, and also with a compote of oranges or other fruits, either fresh or preserved, flavoured with any nice liqueur. Use for a sweet for dinner, etc.

114.—Muscovite of Strawberries (*Moscovite de Fraises*).

Pass 1 pound of ripe strawberries through the tammy, add 6 ounces of castor sugar, 1 pint of warm

water, in which has been dissolved a quarter of an
ounce of Marshall's finest leaf gelatine, the juice of
1 lemon, a little carmine, and a little noyeau; pour
into a mould, and put to freeze for about 3 hours
in the cave. To turn it out, put the mould into cold
water for a few seconds. This can be served with
cream or fresh strawberries, mixed with a little syrup,
coloured with a few drops of Marshall's carmine, for
a dinner or luncheon sweet or for a ball supper.

115.—Little Soufflés of Cheese (*Petits Soufflés de Fromage Glacés*).

Put into a clean pan 3 ounces of finely grated
Parmesan cheese, 2 ounces of gruyère cheese, a good
pinch of salt, a dust of Marshall's coralline pepper,
and a dust of castor sugar; mix with these ingredients
half a pint of strong aspic jelly, that has been taken
when cooling and whipped till spongy but not set,
then stir into it three-quarters of a pint of stiffly
whipped cream and a dessertspoonful of Marshall's
white tarragon vinegar, stir quickly together, put into
a large forcing-bag with a large plain pipe and three-
parts fill up some little paper or china cases, that
have been surrounded with little narrow strips of
foolscap paper cut about 2½ inches wide and 7 or 8
inches long, and fastened tightly round the cases
with sealing-wax. Place the cases on the shelf of
the charged ice cave for about three-quarters of an

hour, then when about to use remove the paper bands, sprinkle over the tops of the soufflés a few browned bread-crumbs, place on the top of each soufflé a little sprig of crisp fresh watercress or any other pretty little light salad, or scalloped cucumber or radish; dish them up on a dish-paper, and use for a second-course dish, or for savoury, or for a ball supper, etc.

116.—Iced Spinach à la Crème (*Epinards Glacées à la Crème*).

Put 2 or 3 handfuls of well-washed spinach in cold water with salt, and a very tiny pinch of soda; let it come to the boil; strain off and press the water from it. Boil half a pint of milk and stir it on to 4 raw yolks of eggs, and put it on the stove again to thicken—don't let it boil; add a little of Marshall's sap or apple green to colour it if needed, and to half a pint of the custard add a small dessertspoonful of castor sugar and a pinch of salt; mix with the spinach, pass through the tammy, and freeze; add, when partly frozen, a teacupful of whipped cream sweetened with a very slight dust of castor sugar. Freeze dry and mould in a Neapolitan box in the charged cave for about 1½ hours; then cut it crosswise into slices about a quarter inch thick, and stamp them out with a cutter into cutlet shapes. Prepare an iced cream as follows: Take 1 pint of cream, 1 tablespoonful of castor sugar, 1 tablespoonful of orange-flower water, and a few drops of vanilla. Freeze it dry and mould some of it in a plain border mould, leaving the remainder for garnishing. When the border is frozen, turn it out in the usual way on to an entrée dish on a paper; place the cutlets *en couronne* on the border, fill up the centre with the remainder of the frozen cream, place a little asparagus or maidenhair fern over, and, if liked, a little cutlet frill may be placed in the top of each cutlet. Use for second course or for ball suppers, etc.

117.—Soufflés of Curry à la Ripon (*Petits Soufflés de Kari à la Ripon*).

Fry in a clean stew-pan about 2 ounces of fresh butter, 2 onions sliced, 2 sour apples, a sprig of thyme, 2 bayleaves, sprig of parsley, about 1 ounce of freshly grated cocoanut and 6 almonds blanched and pounded; to this add a raw or cooked sole or whiting. Fry all until a good golden colour, then add half a teaspoonful of Marshall's curry powder, half a teaspoonful of curry paste, half a teaspoonful of tamarinds, little salt, coralline pepper, and a tablespoonful of Marshall's (white) tarragon vinegar; cover then with 1 pint of milk and cook till tender, add a little saffron yellow to colour, and 3 sheets of Marshall's gelatine. Take the meat from the fish-bone and pound it, and pass all the ingredients through a tammy cloth; add a quarter of a pint of this purée

to a good quarter of a pint of whipped aspic and half
a pint of whipped cream; stir up well together, pour
it into little cases that have been surrounded with
little bands of white foolscap paper in the usual way.
Set them in the charged ice cave for about 1 hour,
then when ready to serve, remove the bands of paper,
sprinkle the soufflés with finely chopped raw parsley
and a little finely chopped aspic jelly, dish up on a
dish-paper and use for an entrée for dinner, etc.

Aspic Jelly for No. 117.

Two and a half ounces of Marshall's gelatine, one
quart of water, a dessertspoonful of salt, juice of one
lemon, one or two bayleaves, two whites and shells
of eggs, a small teacupful of Marshall's (white) tarragon vinegar, one onion sliced, and twenty pepper-
corns and allspice mixed.   Mix up all the ingredients
well with a whisk, and when it comes to the boil,
pass it through a warm jelly-bag, having first run
some boiling water through the bag.   This is made
stiff for borders; if required for garnishing, use only
two ounces of the gelatine for the same quantity of
other ingredients.   By "liquid aspic jelly" is meant
this jelly before it is set.

MOULDS FOR ICE PUDDINGS.

All Ice Moulds are made in reputed measure.

No. 1.—FRUIT TOP.

| 1 | 1½ | 2 | 3 pints. |

No. 2.—FLUTED TOP.

| ½ | 1 | 1½ | 2 pints. |

No. 3.—ROSE TOP.

| 1 | 1½ | 2 pints. |

No. 4.—STEP TOP.

| ½ | 1 | 1½ | 2 pints. |

PRICES ON APPLICATION.

No. 5.—FLUTED TOP.

No. 6.—CHERRY TOP.

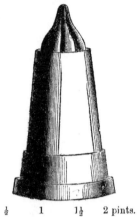

½   1   1½   2 pints.   1   1½   2 pints.

No. 7.—WITH PLINTH.

No. 8.—WITH PLINTH.

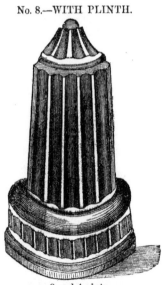

3 and 4 pints.   3 and 4 pints.

PRICES ON APPLICATION.

No. 10.—ROSE TOP.

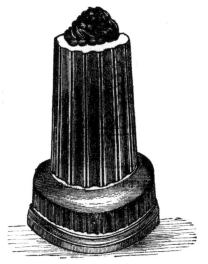

VERY HANDSOME.

2 and 3 pints.

3 and 4 pints.

FANCY SHAPES.

No. 10A.—ICE TRAY.

No. 12.—GRAPE.
(Very bold and handsome.)

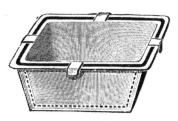

In tin, for serving Sorbets, Fruit, &c.

$2\frac{1}{2}$, 3 and 4 pints.

PRICES ON APPLICATION.

No. 13.—ASPARAGUS.

Height 5 inches, 1½ pints.

No. 14.—PLAIN MELON.

1½ pints.

No. 15.
SMALL BASKET.

Quart.

No. 15A.
COUPE JACK MOULD.

In tin, with lining.

PRICES ON APPLICATION.

No. 17.—OVAL MELON.

7 inches long, quart.

No. 36F.—
BASKET OF ROSES.

1 quart.

No. 36D.—BASKET OF
CHERRIES.

Very Handsome.
3 pints.

No. 20.—WHEATSHEAF.

8 inches high, 1 quart.

PRICES ON APPLICATION.

No. 23ᴇ.—COPPER.

With Cover and Screw,
1 pint.

No. 29.—FISH.

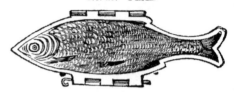

Pewter, 1 pint.

No. 30.—CUCUMBER.

11 inches long.

No. 31.—ASPARAGUS.

8¼ inches long.

No. 32.—GARNISHING OR DESSERT ICE MOULDS.

Grapes, Lemon, Artichoke, Gherkin, Strawberry, Peach, Plum, Pear,
Currant, Corn, Orange, Apricot, Fish, Oyster, Duck, Apple,
and many others.

| Peach. | Pine. | Rose. | Basket of Cherries. | Grapes. | Pear. | Apple. |

PRICES ON APPLICATION.

NEAPOLITAN ICE MOULDS.

No. 33.—TIN.　　　　No. 34.—ROSE TOP (PEWTER).

No. 35.—PEWTER.

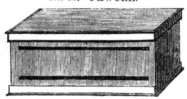

No. 1.　　　　　　　　No. 2.

No. 36.—ICE PUDDING, SHOWING SHAPE PRODUCED.

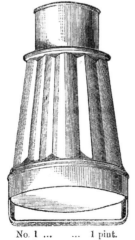 

No. 1	...	...	1 pint.		No. 4	...	...	3 pints.
„ 2	...	...	1½ „		„ 5	...	...	4 „
„ 3	...	...	2 „					

PRICES ON APPLICATION.

No. 42.—DUCK.

No. 43.—SWAN.

1 quart.

2 pints.

No. 44.
DOVE.

No. 45.
BUNCH OF GRAPES.

No. 46.
CAULIFLOWER.

1¼ pints.

1 quart.

1 quart.

No. 47.—HEN.

No. 48.—FISH.

1 quart.

1 quart.

No. 49.
PINEAPPLE.

No. 50.—BASKET OF
FLOWERS.

No. 51.—BUNCH OF
ASPARAGUS.

1 quart.

1 quart.

1 quart and ½ pint.

PRICES ON APPLICATION.

No. 52.—BOMBE.

1 and 2 pints.

No. 36A.

No. 1 ... 1 pint.
" 2 ... 1½ pints.
" 3 ... 2 "

No. 53.

1 quart.

No. 55.—KOSIKI.

1 quart.

No. 56.

1 quart.

No. 57.—SUCCÈS.

1 quart.

No. 61.

1 quart.

No. 59.—BEEHIVE.

1 quart.

No. 62.
ICE WATER CUP.

For making cups of ice
from water, etc. For
serving Sorbets, Punch
Romaine, etc. In
tinned copper.

PRICES ON APPLICATION.

FANCY MOULDS.

No. 52c.

1 quart, and 5 pints.

No. 39D.

No. 39E.

No. 39F.
RABBIT. PEWTER.

2 pints.

2 pints.

2 pints.

No. 39G.
FANCY MELON.
PEWTER.

No. 39H.
FANCY
BEEHIVE.
PEWTER.

No. 39I.
GIANT
STRAWBERRY.
PEWTER.

1, 1½ and 2 pints.

1 quart.

1 quart.

PRICES ON APPLICATION.

Necessaries for Sweet Making.

CARAMEL CUTTER.

To cut 20 squares ¾ in., 5/6 each.   To cut 30 squares ¾ in., 6/- each.
Any other size to order.

WOODEN SPATULAS.

Best Boxwood, 12 in., 1/- each.

SUGAR THERMOMETERS, 12/6 each.

CRYSTALLIZING TINS, with Sweet Fork, 12/6 each.

PALETTE KNIVES (Best English Make).

5,	6,	7,	8,	9,	10,
2/-	2/3	2/6	2/9	3/3	3/9

SUGAR SCRAPERS, 1/- each.

CORRUGATED RUBBER MOULDS, for Fondants.

12 moulds (4 each of 3 Patterns) in one plaque, 12/-
24   „   (4   „   6   „   )   „   22/-
48   „   (4   „   12   „   )   „   40/-

SUGAR DROPPERS, 7/- each.

TIN MOULDS for Chocolates, Fondants, Marzipan, 2/- per doz.
In plaques containing 6 moulds of one pattern, 5/- each.

Smaller Moulds of similar shapes, 1/6 per doz.

MARSHALL'S SCHOOL OF COOKERY.

MARSHALL'S PATENT FREEZER.

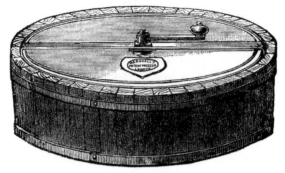

Complete view.

IS PRAISED BY ALL WHO KNOW IT FOR

CHEAPNESS in first cost.   CLEANLINESS in working.

ECONOMY in use.   SIMPLICITY in construction.

RAPIDITY in Freezing.

NO PACKING NECESSARY.   **NO SPATULA NECESSARY.**

Smooth and delicious Ice produced in 3 minutes.

SIZES—No. 1, to freeze any quantity up to one qt., £3.

No. 2, for two qts., £3 15.   No. 3, for four qts., £5 10.

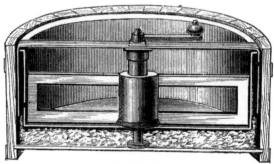

Vertical Section.

Showing the fan inside, which remains still while the pan revolves and scrapes up the film of ice as it forms on the bottom of the pan. The ice and salt is also shown *under* the pan; there is no need to pack any round the sides.

Can be ordered direct from MARSHALL'S SCHOOL OF COOKERY, or through any Ironmonger.

BY ROYAL LETTERS PATENT.

MARSHALL'S PATENT ICE CAVE.

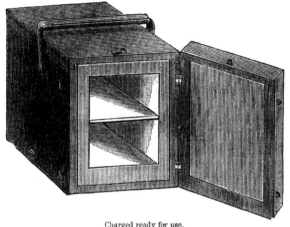

Charged ready for use.

USES.

FOR SETTING ICE PUDDINGS without the use of grease or chance of brine entering, and without the expense of special moulds. Ice puddings when moulded can be turned out and kept ready for use at any minute, so that the ice can be made and held ready before commencing to serve the dinner if necessary.

FOR FREEZING SOUFFLÉS it offers great advantages, as the progress of freezing can be examined from time to time. The soufflés can always be kept ready for use.

FOR INVALIDS to have always at hand a supply of ice or iced food or drink, or for food or drink to be kept hot for any length of time. It is especially useful in nurseries, in the latter respect.

FOR CONFECTIONERS to send out ice puddings, etc., quite ready for serving; for keeping ice creams, etc., ready for selling.

FOR KEEPING ICES during Balls, Evening and Garden Parties, and for taking ice creams, etc., to Races, Picnics, etc.

AND FOR REFRIGERATORS GENERALLY.

SIZE 2, two quart moulds. Size 3, four quart moulds. Size 4 will hold six large champagne bottles. Sizes No. 2 and upwards can be used for icing mineral waters, etc., and kept in dining, smoking, and billiard rooms.

PRICES.

No. 2, £5 5s.   No. 3, £6 6s.   No. 3 Special, £6 6s.

No. 4, £7 7s.

Larger and special sizes to order.

BY ROYAL LETTERS PATENT.

MARSHALL'S PATENT ICE CAVE.

Lid off ready for charging.

When the front door is closed the apparatus has the appearance of a cabinet which can be lifted by a handle fixed to the sides and passing over the top. When the door is open, nothing is seen except the internal cave and its contents (see page 65).

If the interstices between the cave and the metal casing be properly filled with a mixture of two parts ice and one of salt, so great is the cold produced in the internal cave that it will freeze a quantity of water placed in the inner cave into a solid mass, and the temperature produced will stand for some hours at 32 degrees of frost. If instead of ice and salt only ice be used, the temperature in the cupboard will remain at freezing point.

Though Ice Cave has been the name given to this invention, it can also be used for keeping food, etc., hot. By filling the space between the metals with boiling water, a high degree of temperature is maintained in the cupboard. The machine was charged with boiling water at 4 p.m., and a vessel containing water at 140 degrees was placed in the cupboard. At 10 p.m. this water stood at 115 degrees, and at 8 a.m. on the following morning, or after sixteen hours in a cold room in November, it stood at 80 degrees.

Both on the body of the machine and on the door there is a screw plug fixed, by means of which the brine, water, etc., can be drawn off from between the metals, thus rendering it possible to recharge the machine without disturbing the contents of the cupboard. It will be perceived, therefore, that by recharging the machine when necessary a high or low degree of temperature can be maintained for any length of time whatever.

"CONSOMMÉ SILDEEN" Regd.

A.B. MARSHALL · School of Cookery
30 & 32 MORTIMER St.
LONDON · W

DIRECTIONS FOR USE.
Remove the lid, then stand the bottle in warm water in a saucepan, when sufficiently liquid, pour out into a stewpan, make hot and season.

THIS IS THE LABEL (in colours).
Be sure you get it.

CONSOMMÉ SILDEEN

(REGISTERED)

Can now be procured of all leading Grocers, in reputed Pint Bottles.

CONSOMMÉ SILDEEN. No house should be without a few bottles of Consommé Sildeen in the store cupboard, ever ready to welcome a guest or nourish an invalid.

A. B. MARSHALL, LTD., 32, Mortimer St., London, W.

A. B. MARSHALL, Ltd., having extended their long-established Employment Department, are now in a position to offer clients every facility in obtaining :

Cooks (French and English),

Parlourmaids,

Housemaids,

House-parlourmaids,

Kitchen and Scullery Maids,

Domestic and Home Helps (in all capacities),

Lady Housekeepers,

Working Housekeepers,

Cook Housekeepers,

Matrons,

Nurses (Invalid and Children),

Nurse Attendants,

Ladies' Maids.

▣ ▣

Men Servants supplied in the following capacities :
Chefs (French and English), **Butlers, Chauffeurs, Valets, etc.**

▣ ▣

Terms on application to Lady Superintendent, Agency Department.

PURCHASE
The Delicious Preparation
BY
A. B. MARSHALL, LTD.

So Very Useful.   So Delightfully Dainty.   So Economical.

BUY IT.   TRY IT.

USE IT ALWAYS.

Order LUXETTE of any Grocer, or direct from

MARSHALL'S SCHOOL OF COOKERY,
32, MORTIMER STREET, LONDON, W.

F

Ask for "Marshall's" and see that you get it in the boxes as below.

THE PUREST, BEST, AND REALLY THE CHEAPEST.
Do not be put off with any other.

FOR DOMESTIC AND CULINARY PURPOSES.

 Sold only in White Cardboard Boxes, bearing Name and Address.

BEWARE OF UNWHOLESOME IMITATIONS.

MARSHALL'S FINEST LEAF GELATINE,

 Sold only in White Cardboard Boxes, with Name and Address, can in every respect be DEPENDED UPON.

MARSHALL'S FINEST LEAF GELATINE

STANDS UNRIVALLED FOR

QUALITY, STRENGTH, PURITY, DELICACY, AND CHEAPNESS.

MARSHALL'S SUPERFINE FELT JELLY BAGS.

Without seam, various sizes.

Each drum contains a coupon, so many of which (see back of coupon) will be taken as payment for Mrs. A. B. Marshall's books, etc.

MARSHALL'S
HIGH-CLASS
BAKING POWDER.

This Registered Label is on every Drum.

STRENGTH as manufactured, exceeds 120 cubic inches of available gas for leavening purposes, per ounce of powder. Do not be put off with any other.

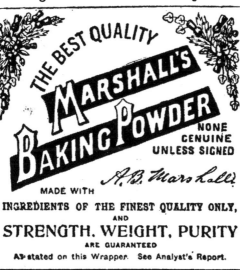

THE BEST QUALITY

MARSHALL'S BAKING POWDER

NONE GENUINE UNLESS SIGNED

A. B. Marshall

MADE WITH

INGREDIENTS OF THE FINEST QUALITY ONLY,

AND

STRENGTH, WEIGHT, PURITY

ARE GUARANTEED

As stated on this Wrapper. See Analyst's Report.

The rights in the above Registered Label are the property of the Proprietors of

MARSHALL'S SCHOOL OF COOKERY,

32 & 30, MORTIMER STREET, LONDON, W.

GUARANTEE.—Every Grocer selling this Baking Powder is authorised to guarantee its purity, weight, and strength as stated. Ask for "Marshall's" and be sure you get it.

In Three Sizes, 1 lb., 10 oz., and 5 oz. drums.

ANALYTICAL REPORT BY CECIL H. CRIBB, B.Sc. (Lond.), F.I.C.,
Public Analyst to the Strand District, London, W.C.

LABORATORY, 136, SHAFTESBURY AVENUE,
LONDON, W., *Jan.* 16th, 1896.

MRS. A. B. MARSHALL.

DEAR MADAM,—I have made a complete analysis of the sample of Cowan's Baking Powder submitted to me, and find it to be composed of absolutely harmless ingredients, the gas-producing constituents being mixed in as nearly as possible theoretical proportions.

One ounce of the powder yields over 120 cubic inches of gas, which is evolved slowly and regularly.

It may in fact be considered an ideal one, having the maximum of strength consistent with keeping qualities. Yours faithfully, (*Signed*) CECIL H. CRIBB.

MARSHALL'S
(WHITE)
TARRAGON VINEGAR

This Tarragon Vinegar is prepared from freshly gathered Tarragon specially grown for the purpose, and represents the highest possible character of production.

This article is the choicest it is possible to produce under the most favourable circumstances, and the price is less than that often charged for the same quantity of other makes.

A trial is sure to give satisfaction.

Order of any Grocer, and see that the Label and Bottle bear the correct Name.

A. B. Marshall's Selected Pure

CANE SUGAR

AS USED FOR

Sugar-Spinning, Boiling, etc.,

Is sold only in Packets containing 3 lbs. net.

(See Name and Address on every Packet.)

It is guaranteed free from Beetroot Sugar, Glucose, or Chemicals.

A. B. MARSHALL, LTD.,

32, Mortimer Street, Regent Street, London, W.

Warehouses : **Union Place, Wells Street, W.**

For the Programme of A. B. Marshall's Lessons,

as arranged for three weeks in advance, see

"THE TABLE"

Established 1886.

"**THE TABLE**" is published twice monthly, and may be had through any stationer, railway bookstall, or direct from "THE TABLE" Newspaper Company, 32, Mortimer Street, London, W., by Subscription, on terms as hereunder.

"**THE TABLE**" contains New Recipes by A. B. MARSHALL, and treats of Household and Table Decoration, the "Cuisine," Menus, Current Markets, Culinary Correspondence and Recipes, and Articles appertaining to Domestic and Household Affairs, and Food.

"**THE TABLE**" is greatly appreciated by all ladies interested in good cookery and other home matters, as shown by the long list of its subscribers, who are to be found in every centre of the Kingdom, and in the Colonies and United States, and it has a larger circulation than any other Paper devoted to similar objects.

"**THE TABLE**" is also taken by the leading Caterers and Hotel Proprietors in the Kingdom, by the Presidents of the Officers' Mess in Regiments at home and abroad, and by the largest Family Establishments throughout the country.

"**THE TABLE**" is larger and contains more matter than any of the Continental Journals devoted to the "Cuisine."

SUBSCRIPTIONS—PREPAID ONLY.

Post Free, One Year, 10s. 6d.   Six Months, 5s. 3d.

Single Copies 4d. each, by post 5d.

INDEX.

A

Almond Cream Ice, 9
,,   Essence, 71
Apple Cream Ice, 9
,,   Green (for colouring), 71
,,   Water Ice, 28
Apricot Cream Ice, 10
,,   Water Ice, 28
,,   Yellow (for colouring), 71
Apricots, Sorbet of, 36
Aspic Jelly, 52

B

Banana Cream Ice, 10
,,   Water Ice, 28
Bartlett Pudding, 46
Bergamot Water Ice, 29
Biscuit Cream Ice, 10
Black Currant Cream Ice, 11
,,   ,,   Water Ice, 29
Bombe with Fruits, 43
Brown Bread Cream Ice, 11
Burnt Almond Cream Ice, 11

C

Cedrat Cream, Ice, 12
,,   Water Ice, 29
Chateaubriand Bombe, 45
Cheese Soufflés, 49

Cherry Cream Ice, 12
,,   Water Ice, 29
Chestnut Cream Ice, 12
Cherry Syrup, 70
Chocolate Cream Ice, 13
Cinnamon Cream Ice, 13
Cocoanut Cream Ice 14
Coffee Cream Ice (brown), 14
,,   ,,   (white), 14
,,   Mousse, 38
,,   Soufflé, 40
Coffee Soufflés in cases, 41
Cranberry Cream Ice, 15
,,   Water Ice, 30
Cream Ices made from Fruit and
     Liqueur Syrups, 8
,,   Ices made from Jams, 7
,,   ,,   ,,   Ripe Fruits,
             etc., 9
,,   Italian, 17
,,   with Spinach iced, 50
Cucumber Cream Ice, 15
Curaçoa Cream Ice, 15
Currant (Red) Cream Ice, 23
Curry Soufflés, 51
Custards for Cream Ices, 6

D

Damson Cream Ice, 16
,,   Water Ice, 30
Dressed Ices, etc., 42

E

Essences, 71

F

Filbert Cream Ices, 16
Freezing the Ices, 2
Freezing Salt, 70
Fruit Syrups, 27

G

Gelatine, 72
Ginger Bombe, 46
  ,,   Cream Ice, 16
  ,,   Water Ice, 30
Gooseberry Cream Ice, 17
Grape Water Ice, 30
Green Colour, 71
Greengage Cream Ice, 17

H

Hints on Making Ices, 1

I

Ice Cave, 65, 66
  ,, Freezer, 64
  ,, Moulds, 53–62
  ,, Moulds and Moulding, 5
Iced Soufflés, 40
Italian Cream, 17

J

Jasmine Water Ice, 31

K

Kirsch Cream Ice, 18
  ,, Liqueur, Syrup, 70

L

Lemon Cream Ice, 18
  ,,   Essence of, 71
  ,,   Liqueur Syrup, **70**
  ,,   Water Ice, 31
Liqueur Syrups, 70
Liquid Colours, 71

M

Maraschino Cream Ice, 19
  ,,   Mousse, 39
Marmalade Cream Ice, 18
Melon Water Ice, 31
Mille Fruits Water Ice, 31
Moulds for Ice, 5
  ,, for Puddings, 53
Moulding and keeping Ices, 3
Mousse Maraschino, 39
Mousses, 38
Mulberry Water Ice, 32
Muscovite of Oranges, 48
  ,,   of Strawberries, 48

N

Neapolitan Cream Ice, 19
Nesselrode Pudding, 44
Noyeau Cream Ice, 20
  ,,   Liqueur, 70

O

Orange Cream Ice, 20
  ,, FlowerWater Cream Ice, 20
  ,, Syrup, 70
  ,, Water Ice, 32

P

Paste Colours, 71
Peach Cream Ice, 21
  ,, Water Ice, 32
Pear Cream Ice, 21
  ,, Syrup, 70
  ,, Water Ice, 33
Perfumed Ices, 28

Pine-apple Cream Ice, 21
,,   Essence, 71
,,   Syrup, 70
,,   Water Ice, 33
Pistachio Cream Ice, 22
Plain Cream Ice, 7
,,   Ice Pudding, 44
Plum Cream Ice, 22
Pudding Bartlett, 46
,,   Nesselrode, 44
Pure Culinary Colours, 71
,, Fruit and Liqueur, Syrups, 70
Plombière of Strawberries, 47

Q

Quince Cream Ice, 22

R

Raspberry Cream Ice, 23
,,   Syrup, 70
,,   Water Ice, 33
Ratafia Cream Ice, 23
,,   Essence, 71
Red Currant Cream Ice, 23
,,   ,,   Liqueur Syrup, 70
,,   ,,   Water Ice, 34
Rice Cream Ice, 24
Rhubarb Cream Ice, 23
Roman Punch, 37
Rose Water Ice, 34
Rum Sorbet, 38

S

Saccharometer, 5, 71
Saffron Yellow (for colouring), 71
Sauce for Nesselrode Pudding, 45
Sorbet, à l'Americaine, 37
,,   of Apricots, 36
,,   of Peaches, 35
,,   of Strawberries, 36
,,   Rum, 38

Sorbets, 35
Soufflé Coffee, 40
,,   Vanilla, 41
Soufflés, Iced 40
,,   of Cheese, 49
,,   of Curry, 51
Sovereign Bombe, 43
Spanish Nut Cream Ice, 24, 25
Spinach iced with Cream, 50
Strawberry Bombe, 42
,,   Cream Ice, 25
,,   Mousse, 39
,,   Soufflé, 41
,,   Syrup, 70
,,   Water Ice, 34
Syrup (plain), 34
Syrups, Fruit and Liqueur, 70
Syrup for Water Ices, 34

T

Tangarine Cream Ice, 25
Tea Cream Ice, 26

V

Vanilla Bombe Dressed Ice, 42
,,   Cream Ice, 26
,,   Essence, 71
,,   Mousse, 39
,,   Soufflé, 41

W

Walnut Cream Ice, 26
Water Ices, 27
,,   ,,   made from Jams, 27
,,   ,,   made from Fruit Syrups, 27
Water and Perfumed Ices made from Ripe Fruits, etc., 28
White Wine Cream Ice, 27

The Importance of Good Icing Sugar

IS KNOWN TO ALL

COOKS AND CONFECTIONERS.

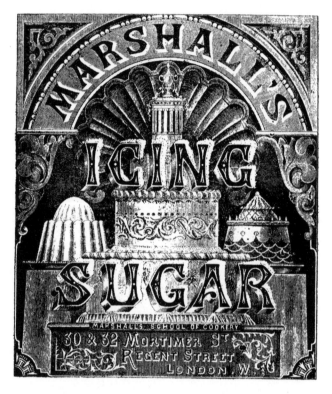

The above Registered Label is on all tins of

MARSHALL'S FINEST ICING SUGAR

Sold in 2 lb., 3 lb., and 7 lb. Tins.

CONVERSIONS
FOR THE MODERN READER

LIQUID

1 fl oz / 30ml / ⅛ cup
2 fl oz / 60 ml / ¼ cup
3 fl oz / 90 ml / ⅓ cup
4 fl oz / 125 ml / ½ cup
¼ pint / 150 ml / ⅔ cup
8 fl oz / 250 ml / 1 cup
½ pint / 300 ml
¾ pint / 450 ml
1 pint / 600 ml
2 pints / 1 quart / 950 ml / 4 cups

WEIGHT

1 oz / 25 g
2 oz / 50 g
3 oz / 75 g
4 oz / 100-125 g
8 oz / ½ lb / 225 g
1 lb / 450 g

LENGTH

1 inch / 2.5 cm
2 inches / 5 cm